UNDERSTANDING AND RELATING TO PARENTS. . . PROFESSIONALLY

BY

ROBERT L. DEBRUYN
AUTHOR OF THE MASTER TEACHER

THE MASTER TEACHER, INC.
PUBLISHER
MANHATTAN, KANSAS
U.S.A.

THE MASTER TEACHER, INC.
Publisher
Leadership Lane
P.O. Box 1207
Manhattan, Kansas 66502

Library of Congress Catalog Card Number: 84-62205
ISBN 0-914607-21-9
First Printing 1986
Second Printing 1986
Third Printing 1987
Printed in the United States of America

TABLE OF CONTENTS

INTRODUCTION

The prospect of talking with a child's teacher often arouses feelings of joy and pride. It also arouses feelings of defensiveness, suspicion, or even fear in many parents. These parents might be surprised to learn that teachers experience the same feelings in varying degrees. Although such feelings are understandable, we must overcome them because, in truth, both teacher and parent have the child's best interest at heart. Therefore, any contact between parent and teacher must be seen as an opportunity to help each other help the child, to solve problems, and to build mutual respect, trust, and confidence.

The role that we, as teachers, play in that relationship is vital. We must take the lead because we are the professionals. Our stance must remain professional always — no matter how parents may react. We must never lose sight of our commitment to the welfare of children, and we must remember that parents want the best for their children and want their children to be the best they can be.

When parents come to us, they are asking for our professional help. They, in turn, can be a valuable resource for us. When teachers and parents approach their shared responsibility in terms of "what we can do together" to help a child, both are building the kind of relationship they both want — and the kind that results in better motivation on the part of students.

This book has been prepared to help you in your efforts to develop mutually beneficial relationships with your partners in education — the parents of your students.

1

THE PRECARIOUS POSITION OF PARENTS

Setting aside the fact that we, as teachers, often feel our position is the precarious one, let's talk about how parents can justifiably feel helpless when they must approach the school.

First of all, let's make it clear that we are not thinking about unusual types of parents. We are concerned with the average, responsible, and caring parents whose children are in our classes. These parents have some common characteristics. These characteristics need our acknowledgment to prevent our labeling all parents whom we encounter as "troublemakers."

Most of all, the vast majority of parents want to get along well with their children's teachers. They will go out of their way to avoid upset. Make no mistake; they don't want to open the door to recrimination. Most parents will do almost anything to avoid making the school experience more difficult for their youngsters. That's why we need to recognize that many parents have fears which often are not expressed.

It doesn't matter whether we pooh-pooh this and say, "Why should parents be afraid?" The fact is that many parents *are* afraid. And, more often than we would like to admit, they may have come to this point of fear because of what has happened to them in the past — either as students themselves or in previous attempts to talk with someone at school. Indeed, many parents feel as though they arc in a precarious, powerless position in dealing with the school. In truth, they are.

IF WE INTEND TO ESTABLISH FRIENDLY RELATIONS, PARENTS MUST RECEIVE A LISTENING EAR

How should parents feel, for instance, when their child comes home after school frightened and worried because of problems with classmates or because a teacher has said, "If you don't shape up, you'll fail"? Or how should parents feel if their child is told, "If you don't have the right clothing, you can't participate in gym"? Let's be honest. Both students and parents are very much aware that teachers and schools *can* carry out their threats.

It is this awareness that can cause sleepless nights for parents and students alike. A teacher needs to ask but one question to see the precarious position of parents: "How would I approach a boss or another adult who made such irrational threats?" Parents can experience strong turmoil after such an incident. They may spend considerable time reassuring their child and trying to get the child to return to school in the morning. They may have to rationalize the teacher's behavior, and say that the teacher probably didn't mean to be so harsh. And they may feel disturbed and angry that such efforts on their part are even necessary. But how will these troubled parents be received if they do show up at the school and want to talk about this type of incident? Unfortunately, we usually don't have to answer this question, because most of them just won't come to school. There's a reason — and it's a good one.

Something in their good sense tells many parents that any teacher who says such things undoubtedly can't be dealt with easily. They fear that such a teacher will most surely minimize what was said — and may put their child in the position of being made to feel like a tattletale and, perhaps, a troublemaker.

This kind of thinking can set the tone for an extremely troubled and fearful year for parents. Parents fear, too, that the teacher may not forget the incident even though he or she insists there is nothing to worry about or discuss further. Yet, we know that everyone's attitude becomes altered after such encounters. Where does that leave the parents? As professional educators, we should be able to answer this question easily.

Often, parents who do go to school wish they hadn't even bothered trying. They may fear that they not only didn't do any good, but have created a bad reputation for themselves with the school. Lucky, indeed, are the parents who can complain to a listening teacher, counselor, or administrator. But too many parents feel as though they are enemies of the school if they dare to make any criticism at all. We can deny these parents' beliefs all we want as teachers. However, we had better take a good look at how we and our colleagues have reacted to parental criticism or confrontation in the past.

The Precarious Position Of Parents

MAKE NO MISTAKE, IT IS
THE TEACHER WHO HOLDS THE POWER

A great deal of power is in the hands of teachers. Parents often feel both powerless and defenseless. In truth, many parents feel that the only safe way to deal with a teacher problem is to go to a higher authority. That's why *how* we deal with parents is so vitally important.

We can do several things when handling parental concerns. First, we can hold ourselves responsible for the things we say and do in the classroom — and respond accordingly. Second, we can respond to parents — in any situation — as we would to anyone experiencing fear. We can begin by adding security to a situation that provokes insecurity. This is best achieved by attempting to solve the problem at hand. Our efforts must not end there, however. Follow-up action on our part, with students and parents alike, is a must.

Our ability to solve the problem is the ultimate test. If we don't resolve the difficulty, parents' worst fears are confirmed and intensified. That's why we need to seek the help of others when the situation warrants it. And throughout our dealings with parents, we must handle our power carefully and responsibly — just as we would expect power to be handled if the roles were reversed, and we were the concerned parents in the hands of a professional educator. With this professional stance, we are equipped to begin handling parents constructively. However, we must also know, understand, and appreciate the rights of parents.

2

THE RIGHTS OF PARENTS

In our attempts to deal with all the changes in society, we're very concerned with rights. Particular attention is being paid to minority rights, workers' rights, women's rights and, lately, children's rights. We can pick up almost any magazine and find an article on at least one of these issues. It's an absolute necessity for us, as educators, to talk about parents' rights.

In the past, the rights of parents seemed obvious and were taken for granted. Our children were ours, and parents' rights affirmed the ownership. As parents we could punish our children — severely if we wished — without interference from society or the law. We could, and still can, give our children religious, social, and moral guidance without interference. When it comes to educating children, however, we have been dealt with differently.

This country has built its strength on the belief that all children should be educated to the utmost limits of their capabilities. Our intention is that every child should experience the benefit of wide-ranging educational opportunities. As a result, parents have had the right to expect society to educate their children.

In decades past, however, when parents left their children at the school door, they relinquished many of their rights. The school became "the parent." Belts and boards were used to enforce discipline. Expulsion was a ready tool for dispensing with the disruptive or obnoxious student.

As adults, many of us can remember being whipped at school —

and again when we arrived home. With few exceptions, there was solid validation at home for what the school did — with few questions asked. Except for periodic report cards, parents heard little from the school. The law read that children of certain ages had to be in school. It was up to the parents to get them there. Often, that was the extent of parental involvement.

THE LAW SIMPLY GIVES PARENTS WHAT
WE, AS EDUCATORS, KNOW THEY SHOULD HAVE

Today, it's different. Many parents aren't asking the school to function *in loco parentis.* Nor do parents allow physical punishment. They want to know about problems involving their children and to have input when major educational changes are being considered. They won't allow their children to be expelled as a matter of convenience for the school. Above all else, they want their children to be educated to the utmost limits. And they want career teachers who understand the educational and personal needs of children. Should these be rights of parents? Most educators think so. Regardless of what we think, however, parents have specific rights under the law today. As educators, we had better know what those rights are if we intend to function within the law.

In all states, parents have the right to take legal action against a school official if their child has been disciplined with an "excessive or unreasonable" punishment. They can also question the supervision of their child, look at records, and challenge those which they believe to be unfair or untrue. Parents have the right to appeal a policy or decision which prevents their child from expressing an opinion on controversial issues. Parents can also examine instructional methods used in research programs funded by the National Learning Foundation.

In most states, parents have the right to appeal a decision that places a child in a class labeled for "disruptive students" or "troublemakers." They have a right to visit the classroom and have a minimum number of conferences with the teacher. Their children can be excused from reading assigned books, studying certain subjects, or attending activities that parents find objectionable on religious, moral, or other reasonable grounds. These are some of the rights of parents as defined by law. As teachers, we must know them — and never violate them or ask others to do so. For example, when we ask an administrator to keep a student who is a discipline problem out of our classes, we are asking the administrator to violate the rights of that student and his or her parents.

THE RIGHTS OF PARENTS
SERVE TO HELP OUR PARTNERSHIP

Our first job is to teach. But that doesn't mean we function in a vacuum. Teaching means many things — including dealing with academics and being sensitive to where children are in that process. It includes caring, encouraging, praising progress, and helping students always to do better. Along with these necessities, we need to function out of a "sense of community" with other school personnel.

Once we open the school and classroom doors, however, we need to move into the larger community, which includes parents. We need to accept that parents have rights — and to be aware that parents' rights sometimes get lost in all the care we must take to uphold everyone else's rights. If we're smart and empathetic teachers, we know that unless we respect the rights of parents, we can't expect their cooperation.

Schools cannot run well without parent-teacher respect and co-operation. Too much goes on in a good classroom these days for it to be regarded as an isolation ward. That's why we should welcome the fact that parents want the right to be interested in their children's education. We should feel no threat from such rights. Rather, we should develop a partnership out of desire — not because it's the law. After all, the children in our classes are more than just our students — they are their parents' children. And the education of these children is a *shared* responsibility. This must be our professional stance. Therefore, we do not have the right to exclude parents — when things are going well or when they're going badly.

Our task is to involve parents, not prejudge them. Then, we must accept their participation to the degree of their willingness. When they are unwilling, we must remember two facts. First, our responsibility to the child has doubled. Second, parents never lose their rights regardless of their degree of involvement, unless the law takes those rights away. Remembering these realities can serve us well in our work with students as well as parents.

3

DON'T
BE AFRAID
OF PARENTS

It's amazing how wild thoughts can go through our minds after a note is delivered to us in the classroom saying that a parent has called and wants to see us. This is especially true when the secretary adds, "He (or she) sounded upset."

Unfortunately, a negative reaction is the most common human response to the unknown. It can ruin the whole day. Perhaps you know or suspect why the parents are coming, and your reaction is a sense of guilt for not having called them. You'll probably spend the rest of the day getting worked up. If you do, the conference may end in a confrontation. Perhaps, however, you have no idea why the parents are coming to see you, but the prospect brings anxiety and nervousness. You may feel a need to be defensive because parents have placed you in a position of insecurity. These are all normal responses. However, if you don't handle your own reactions professionally, real problems may lie ahead.

WE MAY BE ANXIOUS, BUT WE
MUST NEVER BE DEFENSIVE

Even if the reason parents are coming to school is you, don't be defensive. There isn't any reason for you, as a teacher, to fear a parent conference. But there might be a reason for you to feel guilty — if a student's behavior or academic performance was such that you should have notified the parents before they telephoned you.

Regardless, a close look will reveal that if the situation were reversed, parents would be experiencing the anxiety. That's our humanness.

Suppose you had been the one to send the message to parents. They, too, would probably respond in the same manner you did — and probably for the same reasons. No matter who sends the message to whom, it seems to say "trouble." And the problem resulting from a normal human reaction in this situation is this: If the parents and/or the teacher build up negative feelings prior to the conference, the meeting itself will fall somewhat, if not completely, short of success. When teacher-parent conferences fail, student problems are not solved; they are multiplied. However, there are many ways in which you can work for better human relationships and communication with parents.

A note requesting a conference with parents should convey a positive attitude. Your message should be written, tell the nature of the meeting, and be mailed to the parents. Never attempt to solve a problem by telephone if you can arrange a personal meeting. If possible, the telephone should be used *only to set a time for the meeting.*

The best place for a parent conference is in your classroom or in your administrator's office. And don't forget to write follow-up notes to administrators, counselors, and others who might be affected by your meeting to keep them professionally informed regarding upcoming meetings as well as results.

BEING PREPARED MEANS CHECKING WITH COLLEAGUES AS WELL AS HAVING WORK AT HAND

Be physically and mentally prepared for the conference. Organize your thoughts about the student — completely. Even if the conference is unexpected and you don't know why parents are coming, you should have the student's work and records at hand. Also, check with your administrator and counselor about the student's parents. These colleagues might have valuable information you will need for the meeting. Your preparation and organization should reflect your sincere and professional ability and willingness to help the student. This must be your constant professional position.

Your attitude must reflect warmth. You are dealing with children and parents — not things. Lay aside your other thoughts and concentrate on the conference. You must show a genuine concern for the problems at hand.

Don't
Be Afraid
Of Parents

BE PROFESSIONAL — OR YOU CAN'T
GIVE PARENTS THE KIND OF HELP THEY NEED

Present a professional image. Doctors do not begin to shake and
stammer when a patient comes in to see them or they are asked to
explain what they intend to do or recommend. Nor do they show
anger over a patient's X rays. Keep your emotions under control,
unless they are positive.

Likewise, don't make parents feel guilty or ashamed because they
have a problem. Listen to them — and never, never argue. Simply
state what you believe the problem is — without accusing and with
the offer to help. Remember, parents are seeking your professional
help. You are the expert and they should get a secure feeling from
you. You must provide this stability or parents will leave with more
anxiety than they felt when they arrived.

Do not violate anyone's confidence. If you use other teachers and
students as examples, parents will neither trust you nor take you into
their confidence. They'll assume you'll be talking about them as
soon as they leave. Remember, anything you say to parents is likely
to be repeated to their child. Therefore, if you talk about "my unruly
third-hour class," you can expect negative repercussions.

IF YOU DECEIVE IN ANY WAY,
PARENTS WILL BELIEVE YOU ARE THE PROBLEM

Be honest. If you build false hope, parents will know. Present any
problem or praise truthfully and never attempt to deceive parents.
Name dropping, making threats, making promises that can't be
fulfilled, and exaggerating in either direction to add weight to your

case are all forms of deception. Parents may not know their child in the classroom environment as you do, but they do know him or her in the home environment better than you do, without doubt. And they probably know quite a bit about you. If you try to create a false image of the student or yourself, they will know.

You must view parent contacts and conferences as an opportunity to solve problems, build confidence, and learn about students. The primary objective of the meeting is to help a child. It is not to blame others or to feed one's ego. Therefore, you must establish a school relationship with parents that creates rapport and confidence. If you don't, the parents may rationalize their child's difficulty as "a problem we have in our schools." This happens only when we, as teachers, fail to achieve success in our relationships with children, parents, and members of our community. Never forget, the parent conference will also serve as a learning experience for you — if you listen.

During the conference, you may evaluate the situation with the parents, but you cannot judge their behavior as right or wrong. You must sincerely believe — regardless of the home situation — that the school and the home must work together for children. That's why, as a professional teacher, you can never be defensive toward parents. You may feel a natural anxiety with every meeting or conference. But you must know that parents are coming to school to get the help of a professional educator — and you must make sure they are coming to the right place.

4

TOUCHING THE HURT

Our human condition often makes us avoid hurt. If something is painful for us to think about or deal with, we may pretend it isn't happening. Certainly, it's more common than uncommon to fear it or refuse to deal with it openly. That's why we need to acquire the skills necessary to touch the various hurts we witness before the pain gets out of control. If we don't, we shall never really help students, parents, or ourselves resolve difficulties. Rather, we may be consumed by the various hurts, and they may render us ineffective as professional educators.

Certainly, most of us have been faced with a problem situation in the classroom that we wished would go away. In the hope that it will disappear, we go along ignoring the facts as they keep presenting themselves. A child isn't reading well, isn't turning in homework, or is misbehaving, and we hope everything will "work itself out." In the beginning, we choose to do nothing. In the end, we find we *can* do nothing. We have allowed the situation to deteriorate because we weren't willing or able to touch the hurt by pinpointing the problem and involving parents in solving it. Our professional perspective should tell us how grave a mistake we have made. If we look at other professions, we can see how serious this situation can be — for us, our students, parents, and the entire school.

If someone breaks a leg, does a doctor choose to do nothing in order to avoid further hurting the leg? Of course not. Neither does the doctor choose to treat a person's arm to avoid touching his or her injured leg. Yet, this is what we often do in education. When we have a conflict with a student, we may criticize and reprimand — but be reluctant to call parents. Worse, we often don't talk to parents honestly when we do get in touch with them. And that's the problem. We don't touch the hurt exactly where the pain is — and nothing gets resolved. Rather than tell parents the real problem, we may not call them at all. Worse, we may say everything will be okay in time.

Like the doctor, we must deal with the issues directly. A doctor can't set a broken leg without touching it. He or she knows it will hurt. The doctor's responsibility is to touch the hurt in a caring way and cause as little pain as possible in the process. Our responsibility as professional educators is the same — before a situation moves beyond our control.

MANY PEOPLE HAVE BEEN TAUGHT
TO AVOID TOUCHY ISSUES

Unfortunately, many people were taught as children to avoid difficult or touchy issues. It was part of their upbringing. Even if we ourselves were hurting, we may have learned it was best to keep the pain buried within ourselves. Telling adults about our problems only brought more problems. So we learned to make choices. We decided that the best rule for survival was not to touch our own hurts — much less those of others. Mother would say, "If you can't get along with Johnny, don't play with him."

If we have managed to come to adulthood through this system of ignoring our hurts, then we may function the same way as adults. This presents a formidable problem — especially if we are in a position of working with people. Such is certainly the case for teachers.

We should all recognize that there is something we can do. We can change. Admittedly, this is a most difficult thing to do. We may not know how to go about even approaching, much less helping solve, the real problems of children in a caring way. But if we don't act out of our determination to make changes, then we might as well not have found out change was necessary.

When we decide to touch the hurt as professional teachers, we need only remember three things. First, we must make sure we are dealing with the real issues in a professional way rather than a petty way. We cannot allow ourselves any "game playing" here — for this is serious business. If children can't read, parents need to be told this fact rather than given shallow assurances. Second, we need to deal quickly and honestly with problems rather than let them grow.

Finally, we need to deal with the hurts of students and parents in a caring way, trying to cause the least amount of hurt in the healing process. This is our challenge as professional teachers. It is not one we can avoid.

DEALING WITH THE PROBLEM
MAY CAUSE THE LEAST PAIN

The hurts of people do not dissolve like morning dew on a leaf. Like people who put off going to the dentist for fear of pain, many teachers do not look forward to meeting issues head-on. Unfortunately, people often delay going to the doctor or dentist until the pain of not going is greater than the anticipated pain of going. That's a mistake. So it is with us and our handling of the problems of students. But when we do deal with these problems, we may find many pleasant surprises in the process.

Dealing with the hurt often causes less pain than anticipated. Indeed, it may cause much less pain than all the things we usually do to avoid it. Above all, we must recognize that our professional position dictates that we treat issues at their sources. Our responsibility is to touch the hurt in a caring way — remembering that some of the hurt may have been caused by us.

We humans too often function out of our reluctance, when we ought to be functioning out of our love. The times when we will be rebuffed for offering love are so rare that they are hardly worth mentioning. This is particularly true in the teacher-student-parent relationship. Even when it appears that a child or parent is refusing our help, more than likely he or she is merely hiding surprise. We would all do better as teachers if we could give students and parents many more such surprises. One thing is certain. If we decide not to touch the hurt, we won't do any caring. Rather, we shall only pass children with problems on to the next teacher the next year. This can never, under any circumstances, be our stance if we intend to be professional educators.

5

SHARING
THE RESPONSIBILITY
WITH PARENTS

Sometimes teachers assume too much responsibility. Trying to be the sole resolver of all the academic, behavior, and attitude problems of our students is a good example. Though we are responsible for these things, so are parents. That's why we need to share responsibility with them. Not only might our peace of mind be greatly improved, but we might also find that sharing the responsibility with parents produces better results than our efforts alone. The question is this: Why don't we involve parents more than we do?

Some teachers might respond that they don't have time to contact parents. Many think parents don't want to be involved — or will refuse to be. Others think that parents don't care. Some teachers say, "I don't understand parents — none responded to the progress report I sent home," and then add, "Do you know what *my* parents would have done if they had received a letter from a teacher?"

We can't know what our own parents would have done under similar circumstances. But two things are certain. First, some parents don't know what to do. Second, most parents today are doing what parents of yesterday did — trying to solve their problems at home. Most parents believe that once the school has spoken, it's the parents' responsibility to deal with their child. They may do all the wrong things in the wrong ways — or take positive steps which correct the problem. But the vast majority take some action. You might be surprised to find how often parents resort to reprimands as well as "groundings," withdrawal of privileges, and even physical punishments.

Regardless of what may or may not happen at home, a teacher must communicate and share with parents the responsibility of educating and managing young people. We can't really expect to help students unless both we and parents are striving for the same objectives. That's why home action should be consistent with school action. Without such communication, we are like a doctor who diagnoses an illness but fails to give medication or instructions for health care. If there's one mistake a professional teacher must never make, it's prejudging whether or not parents care about their children. If there's a worse mistake, it's doing nothing because of that prejudgment. Remember, regardless of what parents do or don't do, our responsibilities never lessen. Students have a responsibility as well. In truth, however, a student may quit on himself or herself, but we do not have the prerogative as professional educators to quit on a student.

THE REAL QUESTIONS ARE
WHAT, HOW, WHERE, AND WHEN

The real questions for the professional teacher to answer are these: *when* to tell parents, *what* and *how* to tell parents, and *where* to tell parents.

Parents should be told *when* we identify a problem or see anything positive or negative which parents should know. The communication should not be delayed. However, we must be fully informed before visiting with parents. Consulting with administrators, counselors, and other teachers prior to parent communication is a must. Colleagues can be a tremendous help in identifying the problem and aiding in its solution. Before a parent conference, a teacher should know exactly what the problem is, have specific examples to describe his or her feelings or relate incidents, and be prepared to give advice for cooperative home and school action. If we don't know what to do, then we should be prepared to recommend outside professional help.

What to tell parents is *the truth.* That means the truth from both sides of the desk. If there are any unusual factors, such as personality conflicts, let parents know. Remember, you are sharing a responsibility. Parents can best help if they are dealing with truth.

How you relate information to parents is very important. Be tactful and professional, but don't minimize or exaggerate the situation. Never tell parents that you have lost all hope regarding their child. If you have, then you are the real problem. Remember, you are the professional teacher, and you should give parents the feeling that you are willing to help them and their child.

Where you should meet is in a private place such as an office or your classroom. And it goes without saying that you must talk with parents face to face — not over the telephone.

YOU MUST ALWAYS OPERATE ON THE PREMISE THAT PARENTS CARE

As a teacher, you must operate on the assumption that parents are responsible for their children. You must operate on the premise that parents care about their children and have a right to be involved in anything that involves their children. You must also operate on the assumption that contact will be welcomed by parents. If you discover that your assumptions concerning parents are wrong, you must increase your efforts to help the child, because your responsibility has doubled.

Therefore, never prejudge parents. Too, know that lack of time is a poor reason for not contacting parents, because you don't have time *not* to correct a problem. A problem in class is the real consumer of time, both for you and for other students.

If you don't utilize every resource possible in helping students develop, you are not fulfilling your responsibility as a professional teacher. If you don't share responsibility with parents, you have moved beyond your authority as a classroom teacher. Then, not only are you an obstacle in helping children solve their problems, but you have become part of their problem. That's why you must share the responsibility of children with parents.

6

HANDLING
AND HELPING
UPSET PARENTS

If someone were to ask some of our own parents what kind of relationship they had with our teachers when we were children, they would probably answer, "What relationship?" It hasn't been very long since parents simply sent their children to school in the morning and awaited their return in the evening — and that was all there was to it. Parents didn't see teachers very often about their complaints and upsets. In truth, they usually didn't think in such terms. Mostly, parents thought the school was supreme. They just wanted their children to get a good education and enjoy the good life. Today's parents are different. They have a better understanding of education and the work of schools. They know what they want for their children. They are involved, at least in terms of how they think both their child and his or her school should be performing. And when they are upset, many of them come to school. Unfortunately, their perceptions and involvement don't always translate into the reality of what is going wrong for their child.

For instance, parents may want a B letter grade to become an A for no reason other than their feeling that their child worked hard. In fact, they may simply want their children to have A's. But the reasons for parent upsets are countless. They may want us to find a stolen coat or a lost book, and they may be upset because we can't. Or they may want their child to be placed in accelerated classes, excused for truancy, allowed to smoke in restrooms, or pardoned for swearing at a teacher. There are some things we must understand and accept about handling angry or disturbed parents. And right or wrong can't be the biggest issue at hand. That is, it can't be if we want to handle and help upset parents.

We must accept the fact that parents want two things. First, they want us to accept responsibility for whatever it is that is wrong. Second, they want us to act — immediately. We must do both initially, for our task in handling upset parents is also twofold. We need to get parents out of the upset stage and into the cooperation stage in which mutual respect can be established. Then, we need to set the stage for working with parents rather than against them. Though there is no magic formula for gaining such a relationship, there are some do's and don'ts that can give us a higher probability for success.

REMEMBER: UPSET PARENTS MAY
BECOME ANGRY IF NOT ALLOWED TO TALK

Nobody likes to be talked to the way upset and angry parents often talk to others. Teachers are not the exception. Yet, if we handle parents in certain ways, we may win the battle and the war immediately. In fact, we may be so effective that our biggest task becomes convincing them that we forgive their rudeness.

Accept the fact that upset parents can become angry ones if they are not allowed to talk. And they may become ugly if they don't get action. Remember, parents see their children as reflections of themselves. If their children are failing, they feel that they are failing. Too, if their children have been irresponsible and left books or clothing unattended, they feel irresponsible themselves. Likewise, schools rekindle many memories of failure and humiliation for some parents. That's why their initial reaction to teacher and school may be hostile. If you want to break the ice quickly, ask the following questions. You'll find they're disarming. Ask parents, "What do you want me to do?" and "How do you want me to do it." Then after parents respond, you can ask questions such as "What did your child say happened?" and "What can we do together?"

You may think these two sets of questions should be reversed. Not so. Remember, most upset parents come to school expecting resistance or inaction. Many think their child tried, but couldn't resolve the difficulty for a variety of reasons, all of them the school's fault. That's because many kids say to their parents, "I don't know what to do" or "I tried, but nobody would help me" even when they have done nothing.

Therefore, asking, "What can I do?" is disarming to parents. Likewise, you'll be amazed at how quickly parents change their tune when you say, "What can we do together?" "Together" is a great word. It means sharing. It says, "You do something, and I will, too." If parents respond with a request outside the realm of your authority, say so. But also say, "Let's go see the principal and ask for help." Keep in mind, however, that it's very easy to make parents back down, especially if they've let their anger make them look foolish. But this is not your intention or your mission. That's why you must build parents up again once you have made your points through these questioning techniques.

A TEACHER MUST NEVER
RETURN A PARENT'S ANGER

You can handle and help parents who are upset if you don't return their anger or shut the door on their upset. You must set the tone for a permanent relationship rather than an encounter of the moment. Unless you try first to find out what parents are upset about — and be open, honest, friendly, and helpful in the process — you and parents may spend considerable time apologizing for actions later.

Your best beginning with parents is to state your intention to help. You need only to say that you want to make things right for their child. This, of course, may first require your apology for something you did. Regardless, it will always require both your time and your effort — and a willingness to give both. Likewise, it will require not hiding information or protecting your position. Both are forms of deceit.

Once you can get parents out of the upset stage and into the conversation stage, you are really positioned to help and to solve problems. You can if you maintain your dignity and your commitment to the welfare of children. It won't be so difficult if you recognize that upset people are seldom pleasant people. Yet, they can be pleasant once their upset passes.

7

WHEN
PARENTS
GET ANGRY

Some parents are more than upset. They are angry. And they come to school angry. That's why we need to know and understand some realities about angry people.

When people are angry, they say and do things they normally wouldn't. They may even allow their anger to build toward a confrontation. They may *plan* exactly what they intend to do and say. Then, they are likely to "blow up" before they listen to what the other person has to say. Parents are no exception. Our understanding that such behavior is normal does not alter the fact that dealing with angry parents is an unpleasant experience. But such occurrences do not have to end as they began. In fact, they can result in stronger teacher-parent relationships.

SPECIFIC ACTION IS REQUIRED
WHEN A PARENT REVEALS ANGER

When parents come to you in anger, never be defensive. There simply is no need for you to be. Your best initial action is to listen — as intently as possible. If they "blow up," let them. Don't say one word if you don't have to, and never interrupt people when they're angry. When you do speak, always keep your voice exceptionally low and speak slowly. When people are angry and loud, and you get loud or indignant too, the only thing you do is let them off the hook for their bad manners. You will find that if you allow the angry to let off steam while you remain calm, poised, and professional throughout, they will end up embarrassed for their irrational behavior — unless your behavior was as bad as theirs. In truth, if your response is as bad as their behavior, then they can feel justified in what they said or did. That's why you actually support their loss of control if you lose control as well. If you remain calm through the tirade, you'll be amazed at how often complete control of the situation ends up in your hands.

Again, it helps to remember always that parents know their children better than you do. Certainly, they know a different side of their children. Parents always offer a teacher new insights. The truth is that students may be different at home. There are straight-A students whose manners, tact, and personality charm teachers and classmates alike. It comes as a surprise when parents reveal that these students are indifferent, arrogant, uncooperative, and difficult to live with at home. Likewise, there are students who are so shy, quiet, and nonverbal at school that we wonder what we can do to get them to start talking. Later we're shocked to hear parents say that they cannot keep them from talking at home.

At one time or another, we've all seen parents make false assumptions about what is happening at school. Before we have a chance to get together with them to explain situations and actions, some of the beliefs parents hold are going to make them mad. We should hope that they will come to us for needed explanation. Teachers and parents can learn much from each other. That's why, when parents do get angry, you must never return the anger. You'll lose both ways if you do.

KEEP IN MIND THAT YOU ARE
NOT TRYING TO WIN A BATTLE

A teacher must never discount the possibility that angry parents are also scared. They may be afraid they are wrong — or making a bad situation worse. They may be afraid you will "get on" their child because of this complaint. That may be part of the reason a parent is reacting angrily. After parents complain, many actually wait for you to mistreat their child. That is, they do unless you have the skill to handle angry parents.

Too, never discount the possibility that parents may have even told their child what they were going to say and how they were going to "straighten that teacher out." Be sure to emphasize cooperation when talking with the angry parent. Remind parents that together you can solve the problem. Tell them that unless you act together, the child may put home and school against each other. Show them how the child loses both ways when this happens. If you truly believe parents might worsen your relationship with a student, urge a second meeting with both the child and the parents present. Then you can set the tone for home-school cooperation.

Never forget that you are not trying to win a battle against parents. That wouldn't be fair to the student. You must be a buffer between home and school. If you're wrong, don't hesitate to say so. Tell parents you "feel bad about this misunderstanding" or you "didn't realize the seriousness of the situation." Always thank parents for bringing the situation and their feelings to you directly. Finally, always invite parents to call later to see if things are better. If they don't call you, you call them.

RECOGNIZE A PARENT'S SITUATION
EVEN WHEN THE PARENT DOESN'T

The first impulse of parents is often to "take a stand" and come to the defense of their child if they feel he or she has been wronged. If a teacher reacts defensively or negatively on impulse, real trouble lies ahead. Only a professional response can resolve the problem.

Remember, it is parents who are in the real bind. If they don't protect their child when they're brought a complaint about school, their inaction may tell the child that they don't care. If they take the side of the school, the child may claim, "You don't believe me" or "You don't trust me." This fact can influence parents' actions and make them angry. You must explain this reality and commend parents for coming to school on the side of their child rather than not coming at all. Your task is to help parents leave school equipped to function at home better than before they came.

Therefore, try to understand the parental dilemma even if the parent doesn't. Know that parent and teacher have one common interest — the best interest of the child. After the initial remarks have been offered, we are best prepared to resolve a problem if parents are made to realize this fact. This is always our beginning point with the angry parent. But we must mean it.

8

PARENT
PRESSURE

Some can teach for a lifetime without experiencing pressure from others. These teachers feel totally free and have never had pressure or criticism from anybody regarding how to do their jobs. On the other hand, many teachers know pressure well. Students, parents, and even colleagues have taken them to task on everything from grading to class conduct to what they are teaching academically. These are not easy pressures. The weight of pushing from just one parent can alter the whole course of a year for a teacher — maybe even a career. And, in each case, a teacher asks, "What can I do? What should I do? What guidelines can I follow to be personally safe and professionally correct?"

What should we do when we are pressured by a parent? For one thing, we should never minimize the incident. On the contrary, we should always take pressure seriously. Sometimes we don't — and this is our first mistake. And we should look at all pressure from two viewpoints: ours and that of the parent who is pressuring.

In coping with pressure, we must accept some realities and adopt some guidelines. We must recognize the existence of pressure. We shouldn't try to avoid parents who pressure and we shouldn't put them down. They are real forces in the school and the community. And this situation is normal.

We must attempt to defuse a pressure situation. Nothing positive can happen until defusing is accomplished. The best way to do this is to carefully arrange a meeting with a stated twofold purpose: to listen and gather information. We must be open and available to parents who pressure. At the same time, however, we should make it clear that we must examine all information and investigate.

We must recognize that parent involvement in examining, evaluating, and recommending can be very effective. That's why inclusion rather than exclusion must be our stance. Our task is to reveal to them the merits and demerits of their proposal — and how it fits into the total educational picture for the benefit of students.

When we deal with parents who pressure, there are two mistakes we can make which will cause us the most hurt: failing to recognize the influence these parents can exert and being unprepared to deal with them.

We should also realize that in pressure situations it may be difficult to be objective. That's why it may be wise not to make our analysis, evaluation, or decision alone. In truth, we should seek the help of other teachers, counselors, and administrators when analyzing and handling parent pressure. They can help us be objective. And it's not necessary to hang our case on the input and opinion of one person. Rather, we should seek at least three opinions, including those of both teachers and administrators. Many of our parent pressures would be eliminated if we would choose to do one thing following our decision: We should move in one direction or the other. We must never choose to do nothing.

ALL PARENT PRESSURE REQUIRES
TEACHER ACTION

If we decide not to change our position, we should say so. We should also ask a parent to give us time before passing any judgment. We can't guarantee to convert a parent to our point of view, of course, but we may at least get the parent pressuring us to understand our reasons for doing what we have decided to do. Regardless, we must respond and act. We cannot procrastinate. We cannot ignore. We cannot refuse to consider. We must do something. If we don't, both our tensions and the steam of the parent pressuring us may mount. The longer someone waits for our decision, the worse the situation will get for us both.

Though all parent pressures are serious, it would be untrue not to admit that we must also consider the source. Some parent complaints and their sources are more valid than others. Some complaints are more important than others. And we often need resources to help us make decisions. Too, there are times when we may be unaware of a policy or procedure which would indicate that compliance with a request is a must. To be bullheaded and wrong is a position we never want to occupy.

Responding to all student and staff pressures is a must. This is not to suggest minimizing parent pressures, but to make the point that the pressures within the school may have more merit. The fact remains that if we are getting pressure from inside the school, we can almost always count on pressure coming from other places very quickly. That's the reality of internal pressures. It's only a matter of time until they breed external pressures — and vice versa. Remember, people outside the school often have a direct line into the classroom through others — and people inside the school often have a direct line outside.

Experience should also tell us that students and staff will be the last to pressure us directly. After all, students are reluctant because they don't want to get into trouble. Colleagues don't want anyone minding their business — so they won't mind anyone else's. That's why we can't count any internal pressure from students or staff as insignificant.

WE MUST LEAN ON OUR
PROFESSIONALISM AND OUR ETHICS

Some pressures within our working lives are easier to handle than others. For instance, some pressures concern meeting deadlines, completing reports, and following policy. We can learn to handle these kinds of pressures by planning. We can arrange our work in ways that accommodate these pressures. Unfortunately, this isn't so with parent pressure.

Yet, schools have always had to deal with the pressure groups within the community. Sometimes charitable organizations feel that they should have access to the schools in order to gain attention for their cause. Sometimes industries make documentaries on subjects that are dear to their hearts and want the advertising that goes with presenting them to children. And local groups often want to exert influence in none-too-subtle ways. All these can be handled, for they're questions of institution meeting the needs of institution. There is more room for negotiation with these kinds of pressures than there is with some kinds of individual parent pressure on a teacher.

Parent
Pressure

Parents often get the impression that they should have a direct line into the classroom for communicating their desires. People say they believe in academic freedom, but often they do so only as long as there are no conflicts with their own set of interests or standards. When this happens, pressure is often exerted. Usually this means that an individual teacher is involved. It's at this point that the teacher has to call upon his or her professionalism and lean heavily on ethics. One thing is certain — to do nothing is to abandon both our professionalism and our ethics. Action rather than inaction is the best way to handle parent pressures, as well as make sure they don't intensify. And when we take action, we must make sure that our decision-making guidepost is the best interests of students.

9

DRESS
FOR
RESPECT

If we resent somebody talking to us about such matters as dress, we might be wise to put our resentments in our pockets. Whether we want to admit it or not, our appearance affects how we are perceived and received by parents in very definite ways. As professional educators, we need to look at this subject closely, for we have become very casual in recent years. We need to realize that whenever standards change quickly, and the pendulum of expectations goes from one extreme to another, we may find that something important has been lost in the transition. So it may be regarding teacher dress.

There's a book by John T. Molloy titled *Dress for Success,* in both women's and men's editions. It's the result of years of study. Mr. Molloy is a former teacher. In fact, he began his research on the connection between dress and respect while he was teaching. His research wasn't concerned with students liking a teacher. His concern was with the effects of clothing on learning.

HOW WE DRESS IS NOT
A TRIVIAL MATTER

His work shows clearly that clothing is neither a trivial nor a frivolous matter. Instead, just as grammar separates socio-economic classes, so does clothing. A person who uses "he don't" is considered uneducated. Mr. Molloy says there are equally strong assumptions associated with clothing.

Mr. Molloy's research reveals that clothing worn by teachers affects the work, attitudes, and discipline of pupils. If this is so, then teachers' dress affects parents as well. After all, many see professionals daily in the world of work and make comparisons. Molloy's recommendations are these: suits and ties for men and business suits for women. Casual and sport clothes are not recommended. That is, they aren't if teachers want respect. Neither are bold plaids and bright or loud colors. Instead, dark blues and grays are recommended. The next best color is beige. Surprisingly, the color which produces a very negative reaction is green.

Mr. Molloy did a study which showed that women teachers in their forties and fifties wearing soft, feminine clothes were considered positive, authoritative mother figures by students. However, young teachers similarly dressed had trouble controlling classes. Another warning: New, young teachers who wear "in style" clothing won't establish an appearance of authority. Students may "like" these teachers, but they won't respect them, because students actually view such a teacher as one of their peers.

One of the biggest points made in the text is that the clothing people respect is not necessarily the clothing they like. In other words, you may need clothing for your personal life and clothing for your professional life if you want respect. Finally, Mr. Molloy says that if you are dressed in the current "in" look when presenting a new idea to colleagues, superiors, or parents, you're in trouble. You're risking failure because your appearance suggests something other than knowledge and competence.*

THE RESEARCH IS
WORTH OUR CONSIDERATION

Business has long been concerned with dress. In truth, nobody who holds a leadership position and must motivate others can discount the connection between business success and dress. For a teacher, the effect of clothing on establishing respect can be overwhelming. And respect is something we must have.

*See John T. Molloy, *Dress For Success* (New York: Warner Books, Inc., 1976).

Mr. Molloy's work pertains to dress and its effect upon respect, credibility, acceptance, and authority. As educators, we need to use all four of these assets with everyone with whom we must relate — students, colleagues, administrators, and parents. Likewise, we must have these four feelings within ourselves — both in and out of the classroom. It's easy to see why.

Make no mistake, we judge others by their dress, and they judge us, too. If we doubt the effect clothing has on us, we can experiment. Try cashing a check in a department store where you are not known. Try it once wearing business clothes, and again wearing casual clothes. Try the same experiment in a bank or a social situation. If you still doubt the importance of dress, try the same experiment in your own classroom. You might also ask yourself, "How do I dress when I want to impress someone?" Remember, we are all conditioned by our environment. The clothing we wear is an integral part of that environment.

CLOTHING IS SIMPLY AN
EXTENSION OF PROFESSIONALISM

What we wear to school or to a parent conference doesn't alter the state of our minds. Teachers' abilities are not affected by what they have on their backs. We can be dressed up and still have no substance. That is not the point. The point is that people can't overlook our appearance. Vision is a powerful sense, and people are affected by how we look. Parents are no exception.

If we dress up our bodies along with our minds, we can be more effective in influencing people, including parents. There is no separation between body and mind if we consider that we, as educators, are the sum of all our parts. Being mature and professional in how we dress may be just as important as being mature and professional in how we think.

The world of work being what it is, it's of real value for children to see that there are differences between dressing for work and dressing for play. We won't be helping to encourage awareness of these differences unless we seem to know them ourselves. And we may hurt our relationships with students if we don't practice such distinctions. After all, students see how their mothers and fathers go to their jobs each day — and they make comparisons. Just as these realities apply to our work with students, they apply to our contacts with parents as well. Make no mistake about this fact. Considering

Dress
For
Respect

the responsibility teachers have, gaining and keeping student respect cannot be taken lightly. That's why we cannot afford to overlook our appearance. Clothing may not make a person, but it surely can be a contributing factor in unmaking him or her. Whenever we have contact with parents, we would be wise to remember these facts.

PREPARING FOR
A CONFERENCE
WITH PARENTS

So many student problems would find quicker solutions if they were approached by teachers and parents working together as a team. One needs to reinforce the other. When a problem does occur or when we see the beginning of an unacceptable habit developing we should take the initiative to discuss the situation with the parents — immediately.

Often, parents may be unaware of the fact that their child repeatedly fights enroute to school. They may not know that their son or daughter refuses to eat anything except dessert from the school lunch every day. Parents may not realize that their child openly defies school authorities. Generally speaking, parents believe that "no news is good news." Even if similar problems are occurring at home — and they usually are — parents are likely to think that their children are "fine" once they get to school.

Too often, we wait too long before contacting parents. Parent conferences are often our last approach when they should be the first avenue we travel to seek solutions and help children with problems.

Even though few parents are *happy* to hear about a problem, few will disagree with a teacher who tells them quickly that he or she wanted the parents to be "the first to know" so that a situation could be corrected before it became a real problem. Many times, when we contact parents, we offer a long list of things their child has done over the past six months. Then parents say, "Why have you waited so long to tell us?" Is it surprising that parents get defensive about the school's not informing them until the situation appears out of hand?

For the good of the child, teachers must assume the responsibility for fostering mutual support and understanding between school and home. This is accomplished by contacting the home at the first hint of trouble — not as the last resort.

WHEN SHOULD PARENTS BE CALLED?
HOW SHOULD THEY BE APPROACHED?

Yet, a question that faces every teacher is "When should I call parents?" As a general rule of thumb, it is wise to adopt a professional policy of calling parents whenever the question is raised in your mind. Hindsight will usually prove that the question's arising is, in itself, reason enough to call.

When you notice something that you would like to know if you were the child's parents, call or send a note. A teacher simply can't inform parents about a problem too quickly. The real teacher concern should not be when to call, but how to approach parents. Comments such as "I thought you would want to know" or "I wanted to call you before it developed into a real problem" will be appreciated by parents as well as protect you if the situation worsens. But don't overstate the problem. This is easy to do, especially if you are reluctant to call in the first place.

When calling parents about their children, you'll often find that the first sentence after the introduction is the hardest. Here's one you can use on the telephone to encourage a parent-teacher conference: "I'm having a problem with Jimmy and I was wondering if you are having the same problem at home."

This is an excellent approach to use when seeking help from a parent. If the parent says, "Yes," then you can suggest that it might be a good idea for you to "get together" — so that you can begin working jointly to solve the problem.

If parents deny that this problem exists at home, then simply ask them for advice on how you can better relate to their child. In either case, you remain in a position to work with the student as well as the parents.

THE CONFERENCE IS AN OPPORTUNITY FOR
AN EXCHANGE OF INFORMATION

A parent-teacher conference should be an opportunity for parents and teacher to talk together about a child. There are four purposes for a conference: to deliver information to parents, to receive information from parents, to plan a program with parents for improving student behavior if necessary, and to build trust among teacher, parent, and student. If the first three purposes are accomplished successfully, however, the trust is a natural outcome. Usually, teachers plan carefully for each conference so that they can give parents the most accurate and complete picture of the child possible. However, we also need to obtain information from parents about each child we teach in order to provide the best possible educational program for our classes. The following are suggestions for teachers who want to get the most out of their parent-teacher conferences.

Keep a file folder on the work of each student. Grade books and attendance sheets are simply not enough for parent conferences. Seeing is believing. A collection of assignments, test papers, and reports is worth a thousand words. Keep a file for each student, as a doctor or a lawyer would for patients or clients. If parents don't come in for a conference or attend parents' night, then send the folder home at the end of the course or school year. Either way, you will have performed a valuable service for students and parents. In addition, you will find these papers valuable for student examination on the last days of school. Some students will be surprised by what they didn't know at the beginning of school and how much they have learned.

Prior to the conference, ask parents to make a list of questions they would like to ask about their child's progress at school. Note any observations parents make before, during, or after the conference which might be helpful, such as information regarding health, family situations, discipline, concerns, special interests, abilities, etc.

Don't forget to tell parents the time and place and who might be in attendance at your conference. Too, ask them to call the school if they know they need to change a conference appointment at the last minute.

IF YOU NEED HELP
NEVER HESITATE TO SEEK HELP

If you anticipate trouble with parents and want support, don't hesitate to ask your administrator or a counselor to sit in on a parent conference. However, before the conference, the administrator or counselor should be thoroughly briefed about the child and the situation under discussion — including any previous parent contact and the role you expect the administrator or counselor to perform.

Do all you can to make sure there aren't any "surprises" which an administrator or counselor is not prepared to discuss. After everyone participating arrives, you should explain that a colleague is present because he or she is concerned about the student and wishes to be of assistance. Remember, getting help when you need it is not a sign of weakness. It's a sign of intelligence.

Some teachers fear parent contact because they believe that they cannot handle the situation. In truth, the teacher who wants to handle a situation will always contact parents to gain their input and aid. The one who doesn't, won't. Remember, seeking assistance from parents as well as from school support personnel is a teacher strength, not a weakness. However, burying problems under a rug because of fear is a weakness. Never forget this reality.

THE CLASSROOM TEACHER SHOULD
TAKE THE INITIATIVE ALWAYS

Parents who fail to request teacher conferences are often discussed in the teacher's lounge. We pass judgment on why some parents don't come to school and seek us out. However, we usually fail to ask what information we don't have that would explain their behavior. That's why, as educators, we must ask: "What causes these parents to stay away from school?" "How can I reach these parents?" "What can I do to make these parents trust me?" One thing is certain: Unless we show extra concern, make a specific request that parents come for a conference, and do everything possible to reduce parents' fears, many parents will avoid all contact with the school.

Never let a child talk you out of calling parents. And never make any prejudgments regarding home conditions which would prevent you from contacting parents. Sometimes, students will tell us stories and explain why it could be disastrous for them if we contacted their parents. When problems occur in the classroom, your professional responsibility is clear: You must talk with parents. In truth, you have no alternative.

THOROUGH PREPARATION
IS VITAL

It should go without saying that a teacher must know each student's name as well as its correct pronunciation. But it's equally important to know parents' names, too. Check to see if students' and their parents' names differ. You may be in a situation in which you'll be glad you did — and so will students and their parents.

The motto "Be Prepared" is a good one to use when getting ready for parent conferences. Be prepared — to discuss the child's performance on both daily work and tests; to discuss your evaluation of the child's performance; and to point out areas of strength and weakness as you see them. Do not, however, speak for others in a parent conference. Rather, have them present to speak for themselves. Offer suggestions that will show parents how they can help their child, and be sure to explain how you will help their child achieve. Never let parents leave with any of their questions unanswered.

A checklist is a good tool to use when preparing for parent conferences. The list of items to be discussed should include (1) Academics — how the student is performing in each area of study, compared to the total class and national averages, and whether he or she is achieving to potential; (2) Social relationships — how the student interacts with classmates and adults; and (3) Behavior — positives and negatives in the classroom or school setting. Two additional items — emotional growth and physical development — may be included if appropriate. As you report the student's growth or performance in each of these areas, be sure to explain to parents *how* you evaluate.

When planning for a student conference, keep in mind that there are four ways to deliver information or communicate our perceptions about a student's progress. First, we can compare the student's performance with that of his or her peers. We might say, for example, "Tom has considerable ability in math, but his work habits are not as well developed as those of other students with similar ability." Second, we can give parents an idea of how much or how little their child has grown over a particular time period. We might tell parents, "At the beginning of the term, Tom often failed to turn in his homework. Now he is getting it in on time and his grades reflect this." Third, we can convey our assessment of the student's strengths and weaknesses with statements like this: "Tom finds math very difficult and lacks confidence in working with math problems. He does, however, work hard on the assignments and has gained the respect of his classmates." Fourth, we may describe how the student has responded to any special help he or she has received: "Tom has really been working hard on his math since we offered to spend a little extra time with him after class." If there are problems, be prepared to suggest ways the student can improve. Tell parents what you have done and will do, and how they might help. Parents need to know what their child is experiencing and be given the opportunity to follow suggestions. Remember, students usually have the same problems at home as at school. So don't fear talking about problem issues. Just do so in a caring and helpful way.

A CHILD'S PRESENCE HAS
MANY BENEFITS

Sometimes it is a very good idea to have the child present at a parent conference. The effect on the child can be very beneficial. It can assure the child that teachers are helping, not "plotting against" him or her. The child's presence also allows both sides of the story to be told and prevents parents from overreacting when they return home.

Including students in the parent-teacher conference offers many other benefits. The probability of parents getting one story from the student and another from you is eliminated. Whether academic or behavioral, situations can be explained and courses of action decided quickly. If grades are the problem, a teacher can tell both student and parent what must be done, as well as offer assistance and establish times for helping. If the problem is behavioral, it can be discussed from all points of view and guidelines established while student and parents are present. Parents need not return home to talk to their child and then "get back" to you before home and school efforts begin.

PARENTS CAN NEVER BE
OVERLOOKED AS A RESOURCE

It's never too late in the year to have a parent conference. The school year may end for you, but its problems will not end for parents. The summer can easily become a time of worry and waste. In truth, a teacher should have a final conference with the parents of children who have had difficulty or who have failed to show improvement. Recommendations and referrals should be made to help the parents help their children during the summer months. Rule of thumb: If you're worried about a student, talk to parents.

Remember, parents can be a teacher's major resource center. They simply must not be overlooked as a source of information as well as assistance. Parents know their children far better than you do. They have lived with them many years and know their weaknesses as well as their strengths. Most important, they may know what motivates their child and what does not.

Occasionally, you'll find parents who know nothing about their child. They don't know who his or her friends are or what sports he or she likes or even how their own child spends his or her time outside school. Even here, the parent is proven to be a valuable resource because his or her obvious lack of knowledge indicates one probable source of the student's problems.

11

CONDUCTING A CONFERENCE WITH PARENTS

BEGINNING THE PARENT CONFERENCE REQUIRES A SPECIFIC TOUCH

Teachers and parents often view each other as a threat. Teachers may even fear that parents will try to tell them how to teach — and parents may fear that a teacher will look down on them because they have a problem.

When trouble arises, however, one of the best approaches to use is simply to invite parents to a mutually informative talk. Say, "Let's just talk and not try to arrive at any absolute conclusions during our first visit." You'll find parents are much more comfortable if they feel that talking to a teacher will not label their children or bring some immediate action against them.

Many parents are nervous and cautious during a parent-teacher conference. Unless we can set parents at ease, they may relate little that helps us and, worse, they may mislead us.

Conducting
A
Conference
With
Parents

When you have a conference with parents, wait for them in a predetermined place. Don't make someone call you to the meeting. Greet them as you would a guest in your home. Be friendly in a formal way, and prepare yourself mentally to keep the conference on a positive note.

Starting the conference by saying something pleasant and positive about their child helps parents relax. Beginning with a judgmental or negative comment or a sigh and the words "Oh yes, you're Jenny's mother" can intensify parent fears. Remember, parents' reaction may be one of protection instead of assistance if they are ill at ease.

Often, parent-teacher rapport is never allowed to develop in a parent-teacher conference because parents fear teacher condemnation. They enter the conference committed only to guarding family secrets and protecting their child. The wise teacher realizes that these parents usually need as much strengthening as does their child. Therefore, a teacher should never attack parent weaknesses head-on. Rather, offer favorable comments at the outset of the conference. Simple statements such as "Thank you for coming" or "I knew you would want me to call you" can do much to ease tensions and initiate parent-teacher cooperation. Then, when offering a course of action, remember to include parents in the plan and ask them if they agree with the proposed action, rather than tell them what you and they should do.

Many parents lack a true understanding of what really goes on during a school day. As a result, what is a major teacher concern may seem minor to parents. That's why we must take time to explain the significance of such things as curriculum, bus deportment, safety procedures, and hall discipline.

It's also helpful for parents to visit classes and observe activities firsthand. Whatever communication course is followed, teachers are never wise to assume that parents are fully aware of the "whys" and "hows" of teaching children. Communication is a must — especially where problems are concerned.

BEGIN BY
STATING THE OBJECTIVE

In most cases, both teacher and parents go into the conference with the same objectives in mind. If, for example, the teacher intends to deliver a progress report, the parents are usually aware of that fact and come to school with the intention of hearing that report. Sometimes, however, parents and teacher may want to emphasize different aspects of the child's school performance. For example, a parent may be more concerned with the amount of time spent on math homework while the teacher is more concerned with a lack of participation in class. Or a parent may be concerned with a daughter's failure to develop new friends, while the teacher is more concerned about her performance in language arts.

It's always helpful to ask parents what they would like to discuss. If the parents' preference differs from the teacher's, the topic the parents want to discuss can be used to open the conference. Regardless, the objective or objectives of the conference must be clearly stated at the outset. If parents' and teacher's objectives differ, it may be necessary to state guidelines such as these: "Since we have only twenty minutes, we'll talk about your concern for the first ten minutes and then discuss mine for the next ten. If we run out of time, we'll schedule another conference."

Always advise parents, if they are going to discuss the conference at home later with their child, to be sure to present the positive things which were said as well as the negative. Finally, remind parents that the teacher and the parent share a vital common concern — the welfare of the child. With these suggestions, every parent conference can be a more productive one.

Generalizations are of little help when meeting with parents to solve a problem involving their child. Statements such as "Johnny hasn't been acting like himself" or "Susan has been causing lots of trouble lately" tell parents little.

Instead, explain the problem by using concrete examples and specific details. If Johnny has been crying before school, relate this to parents. If Susan has been using inappropriate language in the classroom, share this fact with the parents. Too, the number of times a student has displayed a certain behavior or the events prior to the disruption are of importance and should be offered as part of the explanation.

Prior to the parent-teacher conference, collect your facts and have concrete examples which you may share with parents. Of primary importance, remember to share these facts with an attitude of concern, not as a list of accusations.

Always keep in mind that parents may not be questioning your actions or opinion so much as they are doubting their own. Never discount the fact that parents are worried. Parents have the experience of both past and present. They may have heard the story you are telling them many times. They may have tried everything they know — and failed. That's why they may be looking for long-term solutions rather than what they might regard as a Band-Aid for a minor problem in your class. Therefore, your contacts with parents will be better received if they include help with both the present and the future.

THE RESPONSIBILITY FOR UNDERSTANDING
LIES WITH THE TEACHER

The basis for any person-to-person communication should be understanding. When talking to a parent, we should make absolutely certain that he or she understands what we are saying. Never assume that the parent possesses any degree of understanding about the specific problem. Explain the problem simply and completely. Avoid the use of educational terms and professional phraseology.

Parents are often reluctant to admit during the conference that they don't know what you are talking about. Therefore, you must remember that it is the teacher's responsibility to achieve understanding and rapport during the parent-teacher conference.

Most parents feel that their child's performance in school reflects on them. In order to deal more effectively with parents, you must consider the hurt that they may feel in problem situations. One way to reduce parents' hurt is to help them understand that the only issue is "what we can do together" to help their child.

This understanding can happen only if you are willing to accept part of the responsibility for the problem — and if you are willing to take part in the solution. If you try to stand outside the situation, you only intensify parent hurts. Once parents understand the "we" concept, they're much more likely to cooperate. Likewise, they are better positioned to help resolve the problem. That's because the solution is always a "we" proposition. It includes teacher, parent, and student.

Never forget, many parents are oversensitive where their children are concerned. Therefore, the wise teacher will never do anything to hurt parents' feelings. During the parent-teacher conference, it is wise to point out a child's good qualities before you discuss the weaknesses and failures of the student. This approach will pave the way for a parent to accept criticism of his or her child from you. It will also allow parents to accept your suggestions for improvement.

Too, asking parents for their suggestions concerning ways you might successfully work with their child often makes them quickly realize that you consider the success of their child a joint project between home and school.

WHEN TALKING TO PARENTS, ALWAYS STAY WITH THE ISSUE

Better parent understanding should always result from a conference. That's why you must be careful to keep the conversation on the issue. In addition, be sure to summarize what you have said to parents. Remember two things: First, the parents came to school to work with you in solving a problem which involves their child, and few problems can be solved if issues are skirted by the use of confusing terms or unfamiliar phraseology. Second, some parents may be reluctant to admit that they don't understand what you're recommending. This again leads to an unsolved problem.

Too many times, teachers talk too much during parent-teacher conferences. Remember, one objective of the meeting should be to learn as much as you can about the child through the parents. Give parents a chance to reveal the home situation — even to sound off — especially if they are angry or upset. When listening, don't be defensive. Rather, try to determine the "why" as well as the "what" of their message. There is a difference. Listening to parents can give you many of the answers you've been looking for.

While you are listening, ask yourself two questions: First, does what I'm hearing help me work more productively because it gives me a clearer understanding of the student? Second, does it help me evaluate the effectiveness of my teaching? If your answer to these questions is no, you should steer the discussion toward a more relevant topic. Some good phrases to use in trying to elicit information from parents are these: "Help me to understand ... ," "I'm confused about ... ," "Can you explain to me ... ?" "I'm having trouble with ... ," and "What do you think about ... ?"

If we want information from parents, they must know that we are searching for greater understanding of the student or the situation in order to be of the greatest possible help to the student. Most parents will give information willingly if they know we will use it to help the child, if we avoid discussing "who's to blame," and if our questions reveal that we know we don't have all the answers.

Parents must also understand specifically *what* you want to know and *why* you want the information. A brief, frank statement about the area of concern is sufficient, for example: "Mrs. Brown, Mary often turns in her assignments only half completed. I wonder if you could shed some light on this situation." Be alert for signs that the conference is beginning to focus on "whose fault it is." At the first hint that parents are trying to decide who is at fault, say, "Let's not waste our time trying to figure out who is at fault. That won't help Kim now. Let's spend our time understanding her and the situation as best we can so that we can plan for better success for her in school."

BE SPECIFIC REGARDING ANY
ACTION BEING RECOMMENDED

When holding a conference with parents, be specific about what a child must do to improve. Do not use such phrases as "If Mary would just try," "Danny needs to be motivated," or "We have to improve Linda's self-concept." Such comments do not aid parents in working with their child at home. In fact, these kinds of remarks only confuse parents, and they may end up feeling that nothing can be done.

To really help parents and the student, you must be both honest and specific. After identifying the specific problem, you must tell parents what your expectations for the student are, explain what you have done and will do, and advise them of how they can help. In the process, try to get parents' thoughts about the situation and get them to agree that something can be done at home. Find out whether the student exhibits similar behavior at home, and whether this situation contributes to the problem at school. You should also identify parent behaviors that may contribute to the problem. Obviously, this must be done with tact — and a real concern for both parents and student. Identify alternative actions that you and the parents might take in order to alter the behavior. Then, reach agreement on one specific plan to secure the needed behavior change. Devise simple instructions, step by step, for putting the plan into effect.

In many instances, parents may need help in learning a new skill in order to help their child. They will also need support from you. This may include frequent meetings or telephone calls to check on progress and offer encouragement. Parents must also be prepared for the possibility of initial frustration. They must be helped to understand that, while some changes are easy, most take a great deal of time and effort.

Although you may wish to have parents understand the seriousness of a problem, be careful not to overstate the situation during a conference. Teacher statements may cause parents to overreact, thereby compounding the problem. Remember to discuss the matter honestly, keeping in mind the normal behavior and misbehavior of other students. Don't lead parents to believe that their child has displayed a behavior that can't be corrected, either. If the problem doesn't require the help of another professional, then you and the parents — working together — can solve it. The purpose of your conference should be to plan together a course of action to help the student.

You'll get better acceptance if you make open-ended statements to parents when offering recommendations. Saying, "How do you feel about . . . ?" allows parents to consider what you are suggesting. On the other hand, statements such as "I think you should . . . " force parents into a position of accepting or rejecting the idea. Worse, parents may feel forced into saying yes to avoid your disapproval.

ALWAYS KEEP IN MIND THAT
PARENTS NEED PRAISE TOO

Try not to become defensive if you receive a complaint from a parent about your teaching techniques or methods of discipline. Instead, try to get to the root of the complaint.

Too often, parent complaints are the result of misunderstanding or lack of information. Take time to explain the situation under discussion in detail, remembering that parents may see only one side of the coin — their child's. It is especially important in such cases to ask for their help and suggestions, but remember to do this with sincere concern. Otherwise, your asking for assistance may appear to carry a sarcastic or belligerent tone.

Always try to end these types of conversations on a positive note, with an open invitation for parents to see you again. Remember, parents need praise, too. A teacher can praise parents in any situation for caring and being concerned for their child. Likewise, as teachers we can reinforce the fact that we care, too. Our common concern can begin to patch any difficulty.

When you are conducting a conference, try to avoid taking notes while you are talking with parents. Probably the thing parents fear most is a teacher's judgment of them. Writing notes during your meeting may make them feel very uncomfortable — and may even intimidate them. Too, parents may be reluctant to converse honestly with you because they fear the purpose of your note taking is to reveal their conversation to someone else. Never forget that a clinical situation is not the setting for a parent conference. Make it a positive human situation.

Likewise, thumbing through notes while parents wait during a conference gives the impression that you are neither prepared nor knowledgeable — and makes parents very uncomfortable. Not only will they think you can't talk about their child without aid, but such action is also regarded as authoritarian.

Never do anything that might be regarded as a power play to establish a superior position. The tone and climate which must be created are those of shared concern and assistance. This will rarely be the impression parents receive if they watch you flip through a stack of notes, which they may assume to be a list of incriminations against their child.

During a parent-teacher conference, do not let parents see your gradebook unless absolutely necessary. However, if you must show them the gradebook, cut out a slot in a piece of paper that more than covers the entire gradebook. Then, as parents look at the grades, move the paper so the slot will reveal only their child's grades. Never, under any circumstances, should a parent see another student's grades. All students, as well as their parents, have a right to privacy in terms of grades and other school records.

AVOIDING THE TRAP OF
BEING PUT IN THE MIDDLE

There is one particular situation which may make you uneasy or lead you into trouble. Often, in an attempt to avoid responsibility or to support his or her own belief, one parent will put you in the middle of a husband-wife disagreement or argument.

A teacher must recognize these situations immediately if he or she is to avoid the family-argument trap. These situations usually occur when only one parent is visiting with the teacher. They usually develop with statements from the parent such as "I think you're right, but my husband says ... " or "I try to make Jimmy ... but my wife is always .... " Regardless of the specific topic, you can always see these statement coming. They usually mean the same thing: "Say something that I can use to support my position at home with my marriage partner."

Even though we as teachers can help in these situations, we need time to evaluate and measure our replies. The danger is not in what the teacher says, but in how the teacher's answers will be used by a parent against another parent.

For best results, answer these parent questions or statements with another question. For instance, following the parent's question, say,

"What do you think about that? When have you talked about it? When will you talk again?" If the conversation continues, urge the parent to talk again to the husband or wife and then come in and see you.

This procedure will give you adequate time to prepare for the conference — and even to enlist the aid of counselors or administrators. You know what the real problem is — and you need time to prepare your approach. However, firmly but kindly remind the parent that you, as a professional teacher, must look at the situation only in terms of what would be best for the child rather than what would be best for one of the parents.

CLOSING A PARENT CONFERENCE REQUIRES SPECIFIC STEPS

Don't be reluctant or afraid to approach parents with recommended courses of action. Often, a teacher can most tactfully suggest the action he or she thinks parents can take with a child by posing questions. "Have you considered trying . . . ?" and "What would you think of trying . . . ?" are open-ended teacher suggestions that leave room for parent response as well as action. A flat statement such as "I think you should . . . " sometimes only arouses a defensive attitude on the part of the parent.

Allowing a parent-teacher conference to "drag on" detracts from the impact and significance of comments and suggestions made during the discussion. Teachers who have difficulty terminating such conferences should recognize and remember to employ some closing techniques. Remember, you can seldom terminate any meeting while seated. Therefore, always stand when you desire to close the conference. A statement such as "This meeting has been most helpful, Mr. Jones; I appreciate having had the opportunity to discuss Mary with you. Please do call, so that we can talk again if the need arises" will end the meeting effectively in the vast majority of cases.

However, sometimes even this closing will prove ineffective. In these cases, you must excuse yourself to return to class or other responsibilities and leave the room after extending the proper farewells. This may be difficult for you to do. You may even feel that it is rude. It is not. Never forget that lengthy conversations after the conference tend to detract from the meeting itself — and this is something you must not do.

AFTER THE PARENT CONFERENCE
WE NEED FOLLOW-UP ACTION

Whenever you have a conference with a parent, always follow up that meeting within a short period of time. At the completion of the conference, write down the details of what was discussed, so you don't forget them when writing the child's next report card or when preparing to call the parent for the next conference. Many times, lack of follow-up is a glaring school weakness. Remember, the follow-up is as important as the conference. It proves sincerity.

Too often parent conferences revolve around problems. In fact, some parents' dread of teachers and the school is a result of their having only "negative contact" with their children's teachers. More and more, teachers are trying "positive contacts." This means they call parents when their children have done well with class work or have displayed exceptionally good behavior. Too, it means that teachers follow up conferences about problems with positive comments on the improvement shown by the student. Those teachers who frequently employ this technique for strengthening teacher-parent relationships find rewards for both the student and themselves. Most certainly, it can serve to strengthen parent-child relationships as well.

Don't minimize the importance of teacher attendance at school meetings that parents will be attending. These are excellent opportunities to visit with parents outside the formal "student conference" setting. If you come early and remain after the meeting is over, you can set the tone for later relationships with parents. Meeting with parents is also a professional responsibility. It signals to parents our sincere concern for the students we teach — as well as our awareness of the importance of parents in the learning process.

12

SENDING
NOTES
HOME

Don't jump to conclusions if parents fail to respond to a note you've sent them regarding a problem with their child. Never discount the possibility that parents have taken action at home. Parents may think further contact with the school would be an imposition. Therefore, never misconstrue their lack of contact with you to mean they are not interested in helping their child or they are not receptive to your note. Nor does it mean you should not contact the parents again if the problem persists. Your professional responsibilities never change, regardless of what is or is not happening at home.

Before sending a request to parents, check with your administrator. This protects you from creating a conflict between school policy and classroom practices. Sometimes, individual teacher messages confuse parents and make them believe a school's left hand doesn't know what the right hand is doing. For example, a teacher who gives a student a failing grade because that student didn't wear regulation gym clothes may find this class policy is not supported by school policy. Therefore, the administrator might not back up the teacher's decision.

DON'T SEND FORM NOTES
TO PARENTS REGARDING CHILDREN

Refrain from sending form letters home regarding class misbehavior. Discipline problems should be handled individually. A form letter applies to everyone and might seem to indicate you have lost control of everyone. Excessive use of such letters will cause your professional competency to be questioned.

When a new student enrolls and is assigned to your class, contact his or her parents as quickly as possible. Be sure both the student and parents know your name and how to contact you. Always invite parents to visit class. Ask the parents if there are special situations or considerations that you should know about in order to better help their child.

If possible, set up a time when you can go over all the topics that you covered in prior orientation meetings with other parents. Sometimes, new students are absorbed into a class with only a minimum of instruction and introduction to the school — and parents are forgotten completely. Make sure this is not the case with your students. Such concerns as grading, class requirements, and school activities should be covered immediately — and reinforced within two weeks.

DON'T TRUST THE MEMORY OF
STUDENTS TO DELIVER A MESSAGE

There are a number of situations in which teachers should not trust the memory of students. If a student must bring special supplies to school or needs specific clothes for recess, gym, or athletics, send a note home to parents with specific instruction, so that parents know exactly what they must do.

This applies to all levels, K-12. Too often, parents simply don't have enough information to follow teacher requests. This results in problems and frustrations at home as well as at school.

We are usually good about preparing students for class and activity trips. We need to prepare parents as well — including those helping with the trip. Make sure your parent preparation isn't confined to telephone requests with no follow-up until hours before the event.

If you can't meet with each parent, then send a note covering the following information:
1. Where the class is going
2. Departure and return times
3. The purpose of the trip
4. Exact tasks parents will be asked to do
5. A list of student names

6. Your home phone number in case they have any questions. The importance of preparing parent-helpers cannot be stressed enough.

Not only will this procedure help you, but it also lets parents feel secure, knowing that you are organized. It also shows that the trip is a meaningful activity and has an educational purpose. If all parents have the above information, better home-school relationships will result.

Parents appreciate complimentary comments and private teacher contacts. Notes, letters, and telephone calls can do much to reinforce student interest and motivation as well as create good home-school relationships.

Try sending a short note home or telephoning parents regarding their child's continued excellence or improvement. Too often, parents never know about the high esteem their child enjoys at school. A short note home from the teacher regarding improvement or continued excellence will be most appreciated by the child and parents.

NEVER THREATEN TO CALL PARENTS ...
CALL THEM

Don't threaten children by telling them you are going to call their parents. Call them! Threatening is bad — and twice as bad if you don't call. When you tell students you are going to call their parents and then fail to make the call, two things happen — and both are detrimental to the teacher. First, the students conclude that you make idle statements which are no more than empty threats. Second, a student may, indeed, prepare parents for a call that never comes. Parents can only form negative opinions about you and the school when this happens.

Many teachers make it a practice to supplement report card grades with written comments regarding a child's achievement. Such a practice is well worth the effort since it does much to strengthen the home-school relationship.

However, teachers who write notes on grade cards should keep in mind that comments should be specific and concrete, not broad generalizations which tell parents nothing — or often confuse them completely. Specific comments such as "Did not complete assignments 12, 13, and 16" or "Failed to turn in make-up work after the fourth week of marking period" are much more helpful and explanatory than "Behind in work" or "Inattentive." You will discover that concrete comments can give parents the information they need in order to help their child.

Always make yourself available on the day grades or reports are sent home to parents. Be sure to keep secretaries, counselors, administrators, and office personnel informed of your whereabouts so that you can be reached quickly and easily. Grades, written reports, and teacher comments are easily misinterpreted by parents. Remember, anxious moments can be smoothed out easily when teachers are immediately available. When they aren't, storms can develop overnight.

GIVING PARENTS A
COURSE OUTLINE

Prepare an outline of your academic expectations complete with projects, assignments, dates due, and extra work. Mail the outline to parents, or have the students take it home for their parents' signatures. More than you might ever suspect, this practice will help parents understand course content and expectations for their son or daughter. Many parents appreciate this kind of communication. If a student fails to bring the outline back signed by parents, this fact also tells you something and gives you a starting point should parents come to see you about a problem.

Invite parents to read, and write comments on, work returned to students. Encourage them to help their child with schoolwork — if their child needs extra help. Indicate in your written comments that you are willing to help their child improve daily assignments. This one practice shows parents and students that there isn't any finality to classwork. Even if parents don't take you up on your offer to help, you have something positive to talk about continually with students.

CONSULT WITH OTHERS IF YOU THINK
A STUDENT SHOULD REPEAT A CLASS

If a student might benefit from repeating a grade or class, parents must be contacted immediately. However, a teacher is unwise to make — or want to make — such decisions alone. In truth, most schools have a policy relative to repeating a grade or class. Therefore, talk to your administrator when you believe such action is necessary. And never proceed without consulting with others. It's equally important to meet with parents of borderline students. Be prepared to offer recommendations such as summer school, tutoring, or special assignments. Never call parents until you have a clear course of action in mind.

LET STUDENTS FINISH BY
REPORTING TO PARENTS

Have students summarize their year in a written report to parents. Prepare students through individual and class discussion. Cover each major unit of study, reports, testing, and special events. This practice will help both students and parents recall accomplishments. It is also an excellent learning experience for students. In truth, such reports should be written at the close of every grading period throughout the year.

Sending "state-of-the-classroom" memos is a good way to tell parents what has occurred in the class, what is planned, and which events are special — including student contributions. They can also be used to invite parents to visit the class. If you can stick to a schedule, "state-of-the-classroom" memos can be effective in improving parent-teacher relationships.

NOTES SEEKING PARENTS' INPUT
CAN PROVE BENEFICIAL TO ALL

Taking the time to find out the special interests and talents of parents can provide many benefits for your students. Parents are an untapped teacher resource. Ask various parents to share their talents with your classes throughout the year. This practice will not only improve relationships between home and school, but will also allow children to gain a valuable learning experience — as well as see parents in the role of teacher.

The end of the school year marks a time when many families will move to a new city or state. As a result, many students will be transferring from your school, taking only their memories with them. It can be a traumatic time for students and parents alike. That's why it's a caring and professional gesture to call or write parents assuring them that, in addition to making the regular transfer of records, you will be glad to correspond with their child's new teacher if they desire. Even though this practice isn't usually considered a teacher responsibility, it does take much of the worry out of transferring students to a new school — and leaves parents and children with better memories.

A THANK-YOU NOTE
MAY BE NEEDED

The end of the year is a good time to write thank-you letters to parents and community citizens who have been of special help to your class. Even though you may have followed up immediately after their assistance with a thank-you note, it's a nice added touch to let people know again that their contribution helped make the year a successful one for children. Be sure to include in each note any feedback you have heard from students.

13

THREE TECHNIQUES FOR LISTENING

There are no ifs, ands, or buts about listening skills. They are specific. Listening requires a definite attitude which is reflected in three different techniques. These three techniques are vital factors in becoming a good listener as well as being perceived as one. If you will practice them, few parents will ever charge you with not listening. On the contrary, parents will count listening as one of your greatest strengths as a teacher.

The first listening necessity is obvious. You must stop whatever you are doing when you are spoken to. Look directly into the eyes of the parent addressing you. Maintain this stance throughout the entire conversation. Never let your eyes wander. Likewise, you can't continue to sort papers, look over the shoulder of the speaker, or look at your watch, and still have parents think you are listening. They won't.

Second, you must engage the speaker physically. This action skill is much more important than most people realize. It's easy and much more comfortable to disengage the speaker, and that's exactly why people don't think we are listening. To engage the speaker, lean forward over your desk or bend forward from your chair. When standing, lean your upper body slightly toward the talker. Never lean back when standing or while seated in a chair. Propping feet on a desk or chair is the worst thing you can do. Likewise, don't tap a pencil, play with a trinket, or display any physical mannerism. Rather, keep your body quiet, or it will be a distraction to your listening and the other person's talking. Leaning forward and maintaining eye contact are two of the most important listening skills you can master. But they are not enough.

RESPONSIVE LISTENING IS A
PREREQUISITE FOR EFFECTIVE COMMUNICATION

Though eye contact and physical engagement are absolutes, one more skill is necessary for others to really believe you are listening: repeating in your own words what the person has told you. This final skill actually tells people you're listening. It gives people what they wanted from talking to you in the first place — attention and involvement. This listening skill is called responsive listening.

This skill is not easy to master. That's because you must really *listen* to use it. This means, of course, that you want to listen because you believe that parents and what they say are important. Responsive listening is not repeating or parroting what others say to you. Neither is it telling others how you feel or giving replies which are parallel to what they are saying. Quite the contrary, responsive listening is saying what you feel you heard the person say. Without this kind of empathic responsive listening, you may not be hearing messages correctly.

It shouldn't take a teacher long to think through most conversations with parents and realize that we often fail to be responsive listeners. Rather, we are advice listeners, answer listeners, corrective listeners, detached listeners, and opinion listeners. Maybe that's why parents say we misinterpreted what they said or claim they tried to talk to us, but we wouldn't listen. If we were responsive listeners first, maybe we could move more easily and effectively to giving advice, counseling, supporting, and correcting later. One thing is certain: When we learn to be responsive listeners, parents will believe that we are easy to talk to. Therefore, they will communicate more easily and freely with us.

14

THE
THIRD
PERSONALITY

There is a tremendous responsibility in being a teacher — more so than many of us realize at times. The influence and power a teacher holds in the life of a parent are immeasurable — and should never be minimized. The vast majority of this influence and power is reflected in what is called the development of the third personality. Whenever teacher and parent meet, this personality is developed — in one way or another.

The third personality is that growth which results from the parent-teacher relationship. The outcome of this union is either good or bad. There is never any in-between. If the relationship between a professional teacher and a parent produces nothing, certainly that result would have to be regarded as bad, too. This is a reality that must never leave the mind of the professional teacher.

Of course, third-personality development is not limited to teachers' relationships. There is the third-personality development that is the result of the child-parent relationship. Too, we are all aware of the effect one child can have on another. One particular student may be strengthened or weakened by a friend. We all know children who act differently when they are with certain friends.

The same is true in adulthood. We have seen people "come into their own" after marriage. We have seen the opposite effect, too. This is what makes the development of the third personality through the parent-teacher relationship so vitally important. As professional teachers, we must assume that our associaton will always promote the positive, the strength side of the third personality. What a parent may be unable to do alone, he or she can do when joined with a teacher. It is this communion that makes both teacher and parent able to help children realize their potential.

THE RESULT OF OUR CONTACT WITH PARENTS CONTAINS POSITIVE AND NEGATIVE POSSIBILITIES

While writing *In Cold Blood,* Truman Capote lived in Kansas for a considerable time, there learning about two young men who slaughtered an entire family. He worked long and hard at trying to understand what went into their joint decision to commit such a senseless, violent crime. After reading his book, one can't help concluding that neither of these people would have committed this crime alone — but together they created a third personality. There it is. Weakness met weakness and had its moment of violent spin-off through this third personality.

It happens all the time. Only the degree varies. Either weakness meets weakness or hidden strength emerges to meld with another strength. In either case, there is an explosion for good or bad, and teachers see living examples of this every day throughout their careers in working with children. Yet, teachers need to understand that they themselves cause a third personality — for good or bad. It is inherent in the parent-teacher relationship. If we come to understand that such connections result in forming a third personality and that this third personality is quite real, then we can have some control over its development. A teacher must help to put the third personality to work positively and direct its energies into useful channels with parents — and for good reason. When both we and parents merge our efforts for the benefit of children, magnificent results can occur for children. And good results occur for us and parents as well.